PARALLEL LIVES

• • • • • • • • • • • • • • •

An illustrated

LATIN COURSE

for ALL

• • • • • • • • • • • • • • •

WORKBOOK I

Nevena D. Gilbert

KLAVISOL
Linguistica

MMXVI

Klavisol Linguistica (www.parallellives.org.uk)

First Published 2016

ISBN-13: 978-0-9957613-0-8

Also available on Kindle

Table of Contents

....

i: Preface to the Teacher

pagina I: Table of Contents: Part One

paginae II-XII: Part One

paginae XIII-XIV: Part One Overview

pagina XV-: Table of Contents: Part Two

paginae XVI-XXII: Part Two

paginae XXIII-XXVIII: Revision Sheets

paginae XXIX-XXX: Running Vocabulary for Workbook I

PREFACE to the teacher

This workbook has been designed to complement, enhance and develop the themes already introduced in the textbook. These include Roman education and writing tools, slavery, Roman names and inscriptions, the Graeco-Roman Pantheon, Saturnalia, gladiators, the stories of Aeneas, Odysseus and Polyphemus etc. The links to the textbook are indicated in some of the titles as 'TB Ref.'.

Resources for the 'Cultural Snapshot' rubrics are left to the teacher to decide on. They are an excellent opportunity for independent research and differentiation. Links and suggestions are available on the website (www.parallellives.org.uk).

The 'Real Lives Fact Files' are intended for independent research, using the websites of the relevant museums.

The workbook is also an invaluable tool providing a variety of ways in which to introduce, practise and consolidate the relevant grammatical structures: from simple gap-fills, to games and cartoons.

Cognate work is present throughout, as is translation from English into Latin. The latter is presented in a palatable way, not only as direct translation modelled on examples, but also through 'hidden' translation focused on functions (such as designing gift-tags and dedications).

The illustrations, as in the textbook, have been done professionally to support and encourage discovery, creativity and discussion.

PARS PRIMA

• • • • • • • • • • • • • • • • • •

(Part One)

PAGINAE II ~ III *(Pages 2-3)*

TB Ref: **In ludo et domi**

(at school and at home)

- **Introductions**
- **Roman Education (1)**

PAGINAE IV ~ V *(Pages 4-5)*

TB Ref: **In popina** *(at the tavern)*

- **Names**
- **Roman Slaves (1)**

PAGINAE VI ~ VII *(Pages 6-7)*

TB Ref: **AENEIS** *(the story of Aeneas)*

- **Homer (1):**
  The story of Odysseus

PAGINAE VIII ~ XI *(Pages 8-11)*

TB Ref: **In regia** *(at the royal palace)*

- **Verba** *(verbs)*
- **Homer (2):**
  Odysseus and Polyphemus

PAGINA XII *(Page 12)*

TB Ref: **In urbe et ruri**

(in the city and in the country)

- **Present tense:**
  Gallus cantat.

PAGINAE XIII ~ XIV *(Pages 13-14)*

'Parallel Lives' Book 1: *Part One Overview*

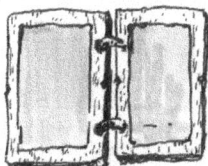

Roman relief from Neumagen, Gallia Belgica, c.180 AD

1   **Translate the dialogue into English:**

Titus: Salve!   ⭐

....

Marcus: Salve!

....

Titus: Quis **es**?

....

Marcus: Marcus **sum**, et tu?

....

Titus: Titus **sum**.

....

2   On his first day at school Marcus is chatting to another boy called Lucius.

⟹ **Complete their conversation in Latin:**

Marcus: Salve!   ⭐

Lucius: ....!

SALVE

Marcus: Quis ....?

Lucius: Lucius ...., et tu?

Marcus: Marcus ....

↱   **YOUR TURN: How would you introduce yourself in Latin?**

3   **Write your own dialogue here:**   ⭐ ⭐

....

....

....

....

....

4   **Answer the question below for each person in Latin** (as in the example): ⭐ ⭐

ⓐ

| Quis est? |

ⓕ

a. *magister est*

ⓑ

ⓒ ⓓ

f. ....
....

ⓔ

c. ....

d. ....

b. ....

e. ....

↱   **YOUR TURN: Draw a famous person.**   **5**

Show your drawing to your classmates. Ask them in turn '*Quis est?*' until you get the correct answer in Latin.

⭐   ⭐

6   **Complete the table with the missing forms of the verb '*esse*' ('*to be*') in Latin or English as appropriate:**

Singular: ⭐		Plural: ⭐	
1. **sum**	'.....................'	1. .... 'we are'	
2. .... 'you are'		2. **estis**	'.....................'
3. **est**	'.....................'	3. .... 'they are'	

ROMAN EDUCATION (1)

Based on your resources, answer the following questions:

1. What was *ludi magister*? ....

2. What type of person usually became a primary teacher? ....

3. Who was the *paedagogus*? ....

....

4. At what age did Roman boys start school? ....

5. Where was a Roman school usually located and what were the possible drawbacks?

....

6. What was discipline like in Roman schools? ....

7. What were the main subjects boys were taught? ....

....

....

8. Why was education important for Roman boys? ....

....

....

9. What skills were girls generally taught? ....

....

10. What are the main differences between Roman and modern schools?

....

....

....

☆☆☆☆☆

8 **Label** the pictures with:

stylus, wax tablet, reed pen, papyrus, *capsa*, ink-well.

ⓐ

ⓑ

a. ....

b. ....

ⓒ

c. ....

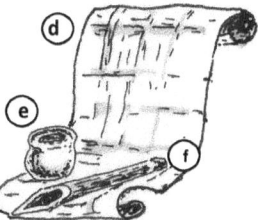

ⓓ

ⓔ

ⓕ

d. ....

e. ....

f. ....

EXTRA 3 ☆

COMPOSITION

Choose one of these short compositions and translate them into Latin:

☆☆☆☆☆

9

1. I am Titus. He is Marcus.

....

2. We are at school.

....

3. The teacher and the paedagogue are also at school.

....

....

4. Pomponia is not at school.

....

5. She is at home.

....

10

1. I am Pomponia. She is Aspasia.

....

2. We are at home.

....

3. Mother is also at home.

....

4. Marcus and the paedagogue are not at home.

....

....

5. They are at school.

....

SPOT THE NAME

1 **In the inscriptions below, find and circle these names:**

Anna	*Euscius*	*Gemina*	*Antoninus*	*Artimidorus*	*Eugenia*	*Asyllia Polla*
Claudius	*Eugenius*	*Caesenia*	*Anicia Caecilia*	*Sergius Asinius Phainus*		★ ★ ☆

a

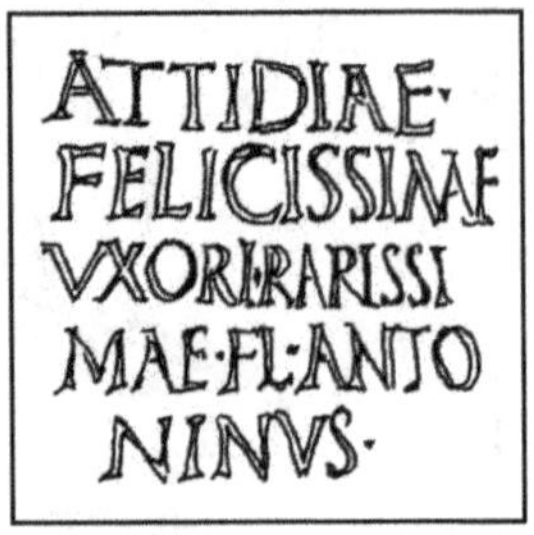

ATTIDIAE·
FELICISSIMAE
VXORIRARISSI
MAE·FL·ANTO
NINVS·

b

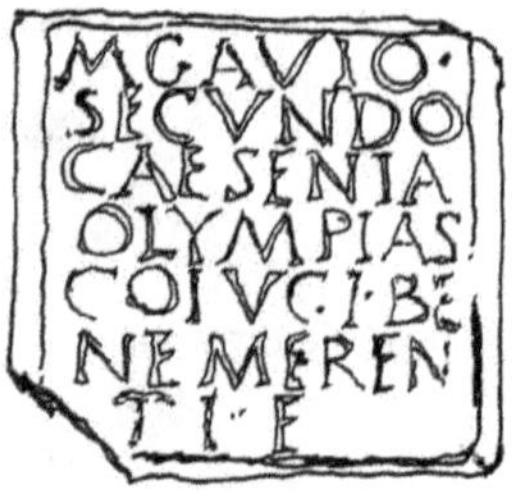

M·GAVIO·
SECVNDO
CAESENIA
OLYMPIAS
COIVG·I·BE
NE·MEREN
TI·E

c

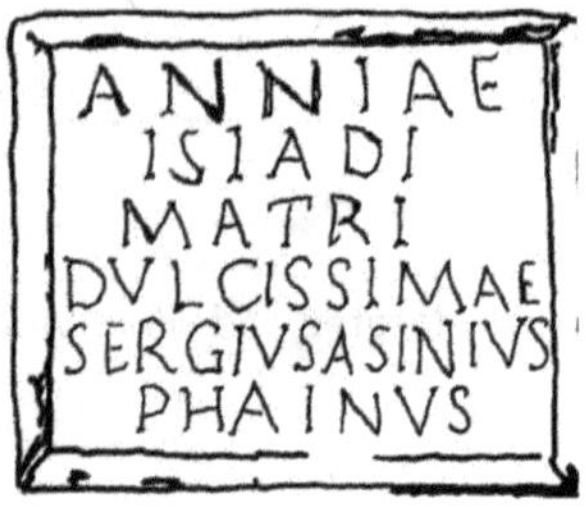

ANNIAE
ISIADI
MATRI
DVLCISSIMAE
SERGIVSASINIVS
PHAINVS

d

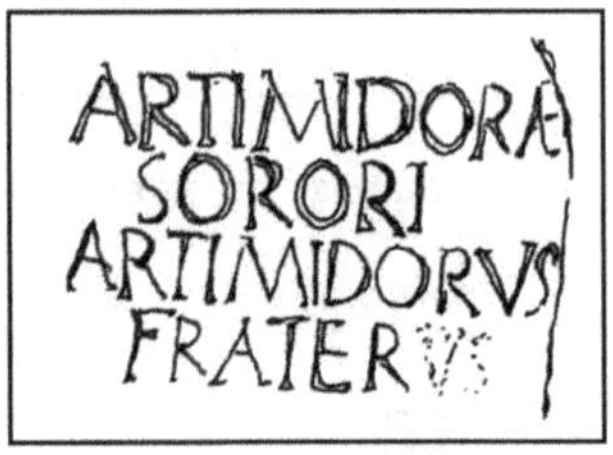

ARTIMIDORA
SORORI
ARTIMIDORVS
FRATER·VS

e

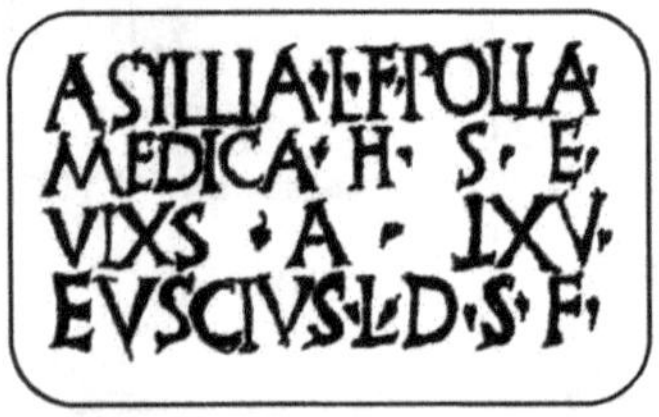

ASYLLIA·L·F·POLLA
MEDICA· H· S· E·
VIXS · A · IXV·
EVSCIVS·L·D·S·F·

f

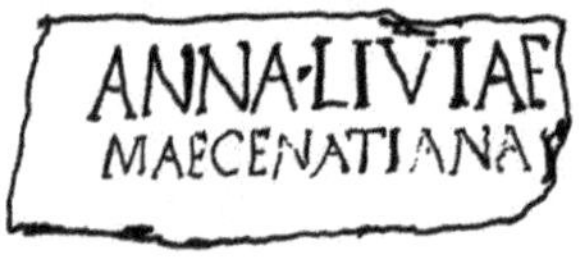

ANNA·LIVIAE
MAECENATIANA

g

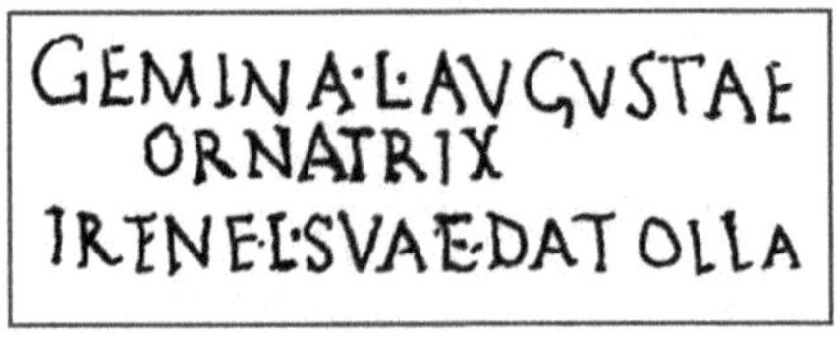

GEMINA·L·AVGVSTAE
ORNATRIX
IRENE·L·SVAE·DAT OLLA

h

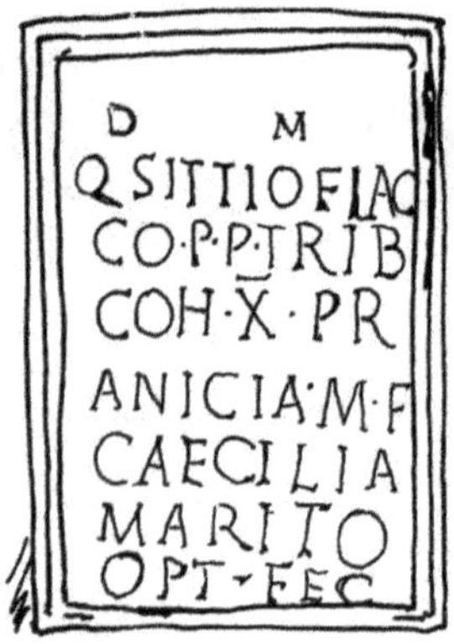

D   M
Q·SITTIO·FLAC
CO·P·P·TRIB
COH·X·PR
ANICIA·M·F
CAECILIA
MARITO
OPT·FEC

i

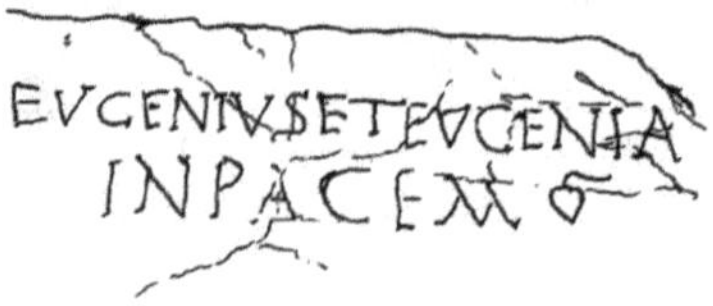

EVGENIVS·ET·EVGENIA
IN·PACE·M·♂

j

APPIVS·CLAVDIVS
C·F·CAECVS

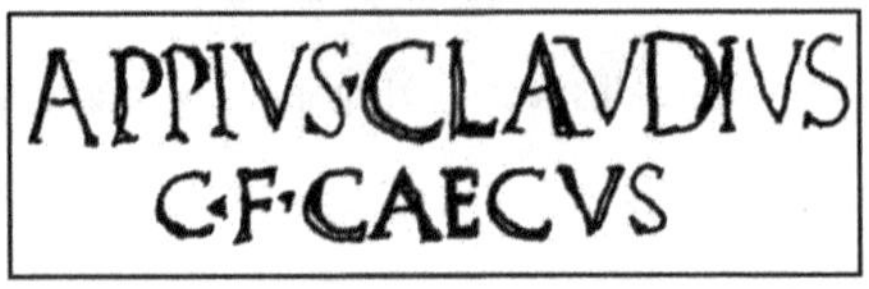

⟳ **YOUR TURN:**

★ ☆

2 **Now sort the above names into groups:**

Men:	Women:

ROMAN SLAVES (1)

Based on your resources, answer the following questions:

1. How did one become a slave? ....
....

2. What types of jobs did household slaves do?
....
....
....
....

mosaic from Pompeii

3. In what way were living conditions different between slaves and masters?
....
....
....
....

4. Think of at least one positive side to being a Roman slave: ....
....

☆ ☆ ☆ ☆ ☆

YOUR TURN:

4 Can you come up with some English words connected to these Latin words?

dominus *'master'* ☆
....
....

servus *'slave, servant'*
....
☆
....

venalicius *'to do with sales (esp. of slaves)'*
....
....☆.

Ruri *(in the country)*

1. Add the missing labels to the pictures: **galli, olivae, porci**.
2. Turn all the words into *singular* and write into the appropriate places, then illustrate.

EXTRA 5 ☆

E.g.

a. (*pl.*) **gallinae**
....

a. (*sg.*) *gallina*
....

c. (*pl.*)
....

c. (*sg.*)
....

b. (*pl.*)
....

b. (*sg.*)
....

d. (*pl.*) **uvae**
....

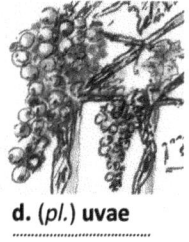

d. (*sg.*)
....

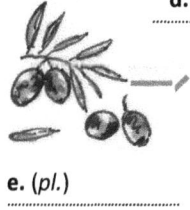

---

5 Complete the table with the missing forms of the words below in *singular* or *plural* as appropriate (as in the examples):

Singular:	Plural: ☆	Singular:	Plural: ☆
1. ancilla	1. *ancillae*	1. dominus	1. ....
2. femina	2.	2. paedagogus	2. ....
3. puella	3.	3. philosophus	3. ....
4.	4. servae	4.	4. servi
5.	5. tibicinae	5. *sumptuarius*	5. sumptuarii

e. (*pl.*)
....

e. (*sg.*)
....

For your **VOCABULARY BOOK**:

tu = you (sg.)
vos = you (pl.)
et = and
quoque = also
dominus = master
serva = slave (f.)
servus = slave (m.)

Romanus *'Roman'*

Graecus *'Greek'*

1 **Dramatis personae:** Connect the main characters with their names. Use the information in your text book to help you.

Dido   Aeneas   Lavinia   Iulus   Anchises   Turnus   the Trojans   the Rutulians

2 **Here are Titus's graffiti in the shape of a cartoon:** Using the code breaker and 'Help Point' in your textbook:

   a. **Transcribe** the text (as in the example).

   b. **Translate** the sentences (as in the example).

a

TROIA DELETA EST.

'Troy has been destroyed.'

b

AENEAS FVGIT

c

AENEAS NAVIGAT

d

REGINA LACRIMAT

e

LAVINIA RIDET

f

PVGNANT

g

RVTVLI RIDENT

h

TVRNVS MORTVVS EST

i

AENEAS GAVDET

j

TROIANI GAVDENT

k

RVTVLI FVGIVNT

3 Based on your work on the previous page:

    a. sort the verb forms below into two groups (*singular* and *plural*)

    b. translate them (as in the examples)

navigat	lacrimat	rident	gaudent	~~fugit~~	navigant
~~fugiunt~~	lacrimant	pugnat	pugnant	ridet	gaudet

Singular: ⭐ ⭐	Plural: ⭐ ⭐
fugit *'he is running away'*	***fugiunt*** *'they are running away'*
....	....
....	....
....	....
....	....
....	....

↪ **YOUR TURN:** ⭐ ⭐ ⭐ ⭐ ⭐ ⭐

4 **Here is a brief outline of the story of Odysseus:** Using the 'Help Point':

    a. **Translate** the story (as in the example).

    b. Draw a cartoon or print out (and stick in) pictures to **illustrate** it.

1. Odysseus ex Ithaca navigat.
'Odysseus sails away from Ithaca.'

2. Odysseus in Troia diu pugnat.
....

3. Equus ligneus magnus est.
....
....

4. Graeci latent. Troiani gaudent.
....
....

5. Graeci rident. Troiani fugiunt.
....
....

6. In Ithaca Penelope lacrimat.
....
....

Help point: ALPHABETICAL

diu = for a long time
equus = horse
ex = out of
fugio, fugere, 3 = I run away
gaudeo, gaudere, 2 = I rejoice
in = in / on
Ithaca = the island of Ithaca
lacrimo, lacrimare, 1 = I cry
lateo, latere, 2 = I hide
ligneus = wooden
magnus = big
navigo, navigare, 1 = I sail
Penelope = Penelope
pugno, pugnare, 1 = I fight
rideo, ridere, 2 = I laugh
Troia = Troy
Troianus = a Trojan

For your **VOCABULARY BOOK**:

in = in / on
equus = horse

fugio,3 = I run away
gaudeo,2 = I rejoice
pugno,1 = I fight
rideo,2 = I laugh

Troia *'Troy'*
Troianus *'(a)Trojan'*

VERBA

VERBS

[*TB Ref*: **In regia** *(at the royal palace)*]

16th century medal depicting queen Dido and Carthage, the magnificent city she was building when Aeneas was first shipwrecked on the shore of Africa on his way from Troy to Italy.

(courtesy of Nomos AG)

① **The Honeycomb Race** ☆☆☆☆

⇒ **Play in groups of 2 to 4.**

⇒ **Choose a *'start'* letter-sun.**

⇒ **Make your way across the board by translating the verb forms on your way, until you reach the same letter-sun marked *'finish'*.** (Write down your translations as in the example.)

A start

gaudet

pugnatis *you fight*

bibis

C start

habitant

venimus

Help point:
You will find a list of all the verbs on page 11!

fugio

ridet

pugnant

dormitis

ambulas

B start

edit

navigamus

dormis

D start

pugnamus

ambulatis

navigatis

fugit

edunt

bibitis

ridemus

C finish

ambulas

ambulant

navigas

A finish

veniunt

editis

ridetis

habitamus

navigo

pugnat

gaudes

A poet compares the building of Carthage to the busy work of bees:

Just as bees in early summer carry out their tasks …

the work glows, and the fragrant honey's sweet with thyme.

D finish

B finish

'O fortunate those whose walls already rise!'

Aeneas cries, and admires the summits of the city.

Vergil, *Aeneid I*
Translation by Tony Kline

2 **Add a group number for each of the verbs below.**

Help point:

Latin **verbs** are divided into **4 groups**:

ambulo, ambulare,	**1**
gaudeo, gaudere,	**2**
bibo, bibere,	**3**
audio, audire,	**4**

N.B. There's also a 'mixed up' one:

fugio, fugere,	**3/4**

(a) dormio, dormire

(b) canto, cantare

(c) amo, amare

(d) doceo, docere

(e) terreo, terrere

(f) scribo, scribere

(g) iacio, iacere

(h) lego, legere

---

3 ➡ <u>YOUR TURN</u>: **Here are some extracts from a foreign Latin dictionary, all containing verbs.**

⇒ **Form their infinitives** (as in the example). Use the group numbers as a guide. ☆ ☆ ☆ ☆ ☆

E.g. dūco, dūxī, ductus ③ I. a) влача, тег-
ля, карам pondus aratri, navem
per adversas undas, equi ducunt
***ducere* ('to lead')**

habeo, habui, habitus ② I. имам
anulum in digito, aliquem in mag-
no honore, fortem animum, febrim,
capitis dolorem, victoriam in ma-
....

haurio, hausi, haustus ④ I. a) черпя
e fontibus, aquam galea; cruorem,
sanguinem проливам; *прен.* ex vano
....

impero ① I. a) *trans.* заповядвам,
предписвам, нареждам aliquid,
quid fieri vellet; *c* ut, *ne* и *само c*
....

in-venio, vēnī, ventus ④ I. a) натък-
вам се на, намирам thesaurum; in-
venimus apud plerosque auctores
....

paro ① I. a) приготвям, устройвам
convivium, copias, bellum, insi-
dias alicui, iter, fugam. b) готвя
....

rego, rēxī, rēctus ③ I. управлявам
equum, navem; *особ.* rem publicam;
legiones командувам. — 2. насоч-
....

timeo, ② боя се, страхувам се, опа-
сявам се aliquem, nihil de bello,
c dat. sibi, libertati за себе си, за
....

habeo = I have
impero = I order
rego = I rule

haurio = I draw out
invenio = I find
timeo = I fear

paro = I prepare

For extra 2 ☆, use the help point and translate the infinitives you have just formed.

Help point

---

4 ➡ <u>YOUR TURN</u>: **Use your work from 1-3 above.**

⇒ **Write down three things you want to do and three things you do not want to do.** ☆ ☆ ☆

VOLO:
✔ 1. ....
2. ....
3. ....

NOLO:
1. ....
✘ 2. ....
3. ....

5 In the table below you can see some of the verb forms from the stories you have read in your textbook.

     a. Fill in the table with the missing forms. Pay special attention to the verb endings.

     b. Translate the forms. ★ ★ ★ ★ ☆

GROUP 1	GROUP 2	GROUP 3	GROUP 4
habito *'I live'* **habitare** *'to live'*	**gaudeo** *'I rejoice'* **gaudere** *'to rejoice'*	**bibo** *'I drink'* **biběre** *'to drink'*	**venio** *'I come'* **venire** *'to come'*
singular	*singular*	*singular*	*singular*
1. habit**o** *'I live'*	**1.** …………………… ……………………	**1.** bib**o** *'I drink'*	**1.** …………………… ……………………
2. habita**s** *'you live'*	**2.** …………………… ……………………	**2.** bib**is** *'you drink'*	**2.** …………………… ……………………
3. …………………… ……………………	**3.** gaude**t** *'he (she) rejoices'*	**3.** bib**it** *'he (she) drinks'*	**3.** …………………… ……………………
plural	*plural*	*plural*	*plural*
1. …………………… ……………………	**1.** …………………… ……………………	**1.** bibi**mus** *'we drink'*	**1.** veni**mus** *'we come'*
2. …………………… ……………………	**2.** …………………… ……………………	**2.** bibi**tis** *'you drink'*	**2.** veni**tis** *'you come'*
3. …………………… ……………………	**3.** gaude**nt** *'they rejoice'*	**3.** …………………… ……………………	**3.** veni**unt** *'they come'*

---

6 COMPOSITION ★ ★ ★ ★ ☆

Translate this composition into Latin:

1. I am a student. *(student = discipulus (m), discipula (f))*

…………………………………………………………………

2. I study at school. *(I study = studeo, studere, 2)*

…………………………………………………………………

3. Do you (pl.) like to study? *(I like = amo, amare, 1)*

…………………………………………………………………

4. Where do you (pl.) study? *(where? = ubi?)*

…………………………………………………………………

5. We study at home.

…………………………………………………………………

6. We also like to study. *(also = quoque)*

…………………………………………………………………

---

7 YOUR TURN: *'Amas studere?'*

• Draw an answer to the question above

• Caption it in Latin. ⟵ EXTRA 3 ☆

HOMER (2): POLYPHEMUS

Based on your resources, answer the following questions:

1. Who was **Polyphemus**? ....

2. Where did he live and how did he make his living? ....

....

3. How and why did Odysseus get him to go to sleep? ....

....

4. Why did his brothers / friends not help him when he was attacked by Odysseus and his men?

....

....

5. How did Odysseus and his men escape from Polyphemus?

....

....

6. What consequences did this episode have for Odysseus?

....

....

☆ ☆ ☆ ☆ ☆

Odysee, esurimus et sitimus!

In ripa spelunca est!

For **YOU**: Odysseus et Polyphemus

Munch, munch...

Odysseus et amici diu navigant.

In spelunca lac et caseum inveniunt. Edunt et bibunt.

Polyphemus iratus est.

Nunc ego vos edere volo!

☆ ☆ ☆ ☆ ☆

Help point:

esurio, esurire, 4 = I am hungry
sitio, sitire, 4 = I am thirsty
amicus = friend
diu = for a long time
ripa = shore   spelunca = cave
caseus = cheese   lac = milk
invenio, invenire, 4 = I find
ego = I   vos = you (pl.)
nunc = now   volo, velle = I
                              want

For your **VOCABULARY BOOK**:

ambulo, ambulare, **1** = I walk
bibo, bibĕre, **3** = I drink
dormio, dormire, **4** = I sleep
edo, edĕre, **3** = I eat
fugio, fugĕre **3** = I run away
gaudeo, gaudere, **2** = I rejoice
habito, habitare **1** = I live
navigo, navigare **1** = I sail
pugno, pugnare **1** = I fight
rideo, ridere **2** = I laugh
venio, venire **4** = I come

☆☆☆☆☆

1 Here is a philosopher hard at work. **Can you translate his wise thoughts?**

a Tempus **fugit**.
E.g. *Time*
....
flies.
....

b Natura docet.
....
....

c Cogito ergo sum.
....
....

d Dei imperant.
....
....

e Pecunia non olet.
....
....

Help point:
cogito, 1 = I think
deus = god
doceo, 2 = I teach
ergo = therefore
impero, 1 = I order, command
natura = nature
oleo, 2 = I smell
pecunia = money
tempus = time

YOUR TURN:

2 Here is some space for your own wise thoughts. (Write them down **in English.**) ← EXTRA 3 ☆

....
....
....

....
....
....

....
....
....

☆☆☆☆☆

3 What is going on in the pictures? **Can you translate the captions?**

a *Tempus fugit.*
E.g. *Time*
is flying.
....

b **Magister docet.**
....
....

c *Philosophus cogitat.*
....
....

d *Gallus cantat.*
....

Luna et stellae splendent.
....
....

Help point:
canto, 1 = I sing
cogito, 1 = I think
doceo, 2 = I teach
gallus = cockerel
impero, 1 = I order, command
Luna = the Moon
magistra = teacher (*f*)
splendeo, 2 = I shine
stella = star
tempus = time

'PARALLEL LIVES' Book 1 : Part One Overview

1 **Answer** the following questions in English (as in the example):

Look for answers on p. 2 in TB

E.g. **Q:** Quis est Titus? **A:** *Titus is a Roman boy, Marcus' friend.*

Q: Quis est Marcus? **A:** ....

Q: Quis est paedagogus? **A:** ....

Q: Quis est Aspasia? **A:** ....

2 **Fill in** the missing endings, then **translate** the sentences into English (as in the example):

Look for answers on p. 3 in TB

E.g. Eugenia Graec*a* est. *'Eugenia is Greek.'*

Pomponia Roman....... est. ....

Ancillae Graec...... sunt. ....

Dominus Roman........... est. ....

Philosophi Graec..... sunt. ....

3 **Complete** Aeneas' family tree with the appropriate names (as in the examples):

Aeneas ~~**Venus**~~ **Anchises** **Iulus** ~~**Creusa**~~

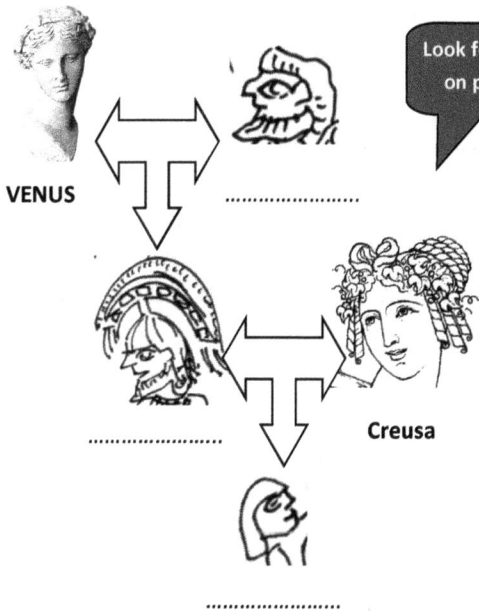

Look for answers on p. 4 in TB

VENUS ....

.... **Creusa**

....

---

extra **Complete** the story with one of the words below, then translate (as in the example):

amat ~~**regina**~~ **regia** **ripa**

Dido *regina* est.

'Dido is a queen.'

Dido in .... ambulat.

....

Dido in .... habitat.

....

Dido Aenea ....

....

4 **Add** a group **number** (1, 2, 3, 4) for each of the verbs below (as in the example):

E.g. canto, cantare, **1** ('I sing')

amo, amare, ... ('I love')

audio, audire, ... ('I listen')

doceo, docere, ... ('I teach')

scribo, scribere, ... ('I write')

Look for answers on p. 5 in TB and p. 9 in WB

---

5 Answer the following questions in Latin (as in the example):

E.g. **Q:** Quid facit dominus?

Look for answers on p. 6 in TB and p. 12 in WB

A: *Dominus imperat.*

Q: Quid facit scriba?

A: ....

Q: Quid facit servus?

A: ....

Q: Quid facit philosophus?

A: ....

---

6 Translate each of the following sentences in two different ways:

Deus imperat.

Look for answers on p. 7 and WB p. 12

....

....

Olivae florent.

....

....

7 Imagine you are **a slave in a Roman town house** *or* **a Roman country estate** (*villa rustica*).

Look for answers on pp. 6-7 in TB and p. 5 in WB

⇒ What do you like and dislike about your life?

You could include:

- your work
- how much freedom you have
- how you are treated
- your hopes for the future.

PARS SECUNDA
. . . .
(Part Two)

PAGINAE XVI ~ XVII *(Pages 16-17)*

Liberi et Liberti
(freeborn and freedmen)

Dei et Deae *(gods and goddesses)*

- **CUIUS?** *(Whose? / Of what?)*

PAGINAE XVIII ~ XIX *(Pages 18-19)*

SATURNALIA

Real lives FACT FILE 1:
A Roman pet dog

- **CUI?** *(Who for? / Who to?)*

PAGINAE XX ~ XXI *(Pages 20-21)*

SAGITTIS
VVLNERATVS
LVXVRIVS

Ludus et Ludi *(School and the Games)*

- **QUO** *(What with?)*
- **Latin derivatives**

PAGINA XXII *(Page 22)*

Cultural SNAPSHOT extra:
Roman Gladiators

Real lives FACT FILE 2:
Gladiator trainers

PAGINAE XXIII ~ XXVIII *(Pages 23-28)*

'Parallel Lives' Book 1: REVISION SHEETS 1-6

Liberi et liberti *(freeborn and freedmen)*

1 Below are some inscriptions - some with the names of free-born men and women and some with those of freedmen and women.

⇒ Use the examples as a guide and:

CUIUS?
(Whose?)

1. **Transcribe** each inscription.

2. **Translate** the full name of each person.

3. **Expand the abbreviations** (use the 'Help point').

E.g.

APVLEIA·SEX·F·

1. **APVLEIA ✦ SEX ✦ F**

2. 'Apuleia, Sextus's daughter'

3. **Apuleia Sex**(ti) **f**(ilia)

E.g.

AVRELIA·L·L

1. **AVRELIA ✦ L ✦ L**

2. 'Aurelia, Lucius's freedwoman'

3. **Aurelia L**(ucii) **l**(iberta)

Help point: ABBREVIATIONS

Stone inscriptions were very expensive, so a lot of abbreviations were used to shorten them, thus cutting the cost.

Here are some popular abbreviations:

Abbrev.:	Stands for:
C	**Gaius** *(the name Gaius)*
CN	**Gnaeus** *(the name Gnaeus)*
F	**filius** *(son)* / **filia** *(daughter)*
L	**libertus** *(freedman)* / **liberta** *(freedwoman)*
	Lucius *(the name Lucius)*
M	**Marcus** *(the name Marcus)*
P	**Publius** *(the name Publius)*
Q	**Quintus** *(the name Quintus)*
SEX	**Sextus** *(the name Sextus)*
T	**Titus** *(the name Titus)*

(a) ANICIA·M·F

1. ....
2. ....
....
3. ....
....

(b) VOLVSIA·C·L

1. ....
2. ....
....
3. ....
....

(c) L·CORNELIVS·CN·F·

1. ....
2. ....
3. ....

(d) Q·CORNELIVS · Q · L

1. ....
2. ....
3. ....

(e) APPIVS·CLAVDIVS C·F·CAECVS

1. ....
....
2. ....
....
3. ....
....

(f) ·P·GESSTVS·P·L·PRIMVS

1. ....
....
2. ....
....
3. ....
....

(g) ASILLIA·L·F·POLLA

1. ....
2. ....
....
3. ....
....

N.B. The emperor's title was **'Augustus'** (abbrev. AVG)
The emperor's wife was **'Augusta'**

(h) FORTVNATVS·AVG·L·

1. ....
2. ....
....
3. ....
....

(i) GEMINA·L·AVGVSTAE

1. ....
2. ....
....
3. ....
....

2 The Romans borrowed many of their **gods** from the Greeks and changed most of their names to make them more Roman-sounding. Below are the pictures of the most important deities of the Graeco-Roman world.

⇒ Do some research, then **label the pictures with the appropriate Roman name**.

NIKE
....

APOLLO   ARTEMIS   ATHENA

HERA   ZEUS

....

3 The texts in the table below give short explanations of what each of these Roman gods was a deity of.

⇒ Use the example as a guide:

CUIUS? *(of what?)*

a. Translate the short texts.

DIONYSUS

b. Fill in the table with the appropriate names.

....

Name:	Job description:
a	dominus deorum est; deus tonitruorum. ....
b	regina deorum est; dea matronarum. ....
c	dominus Musarum est; deus poetarum. Geminus Dianae est. ....
d	dea silvarum et bestiarum est.
e	dea sapientiae, poetarum et bellorum est. ....
f	nuntius deorum est; patronus negotiorum, protector viatorum. ....
e.g. *BACCHUS*	deus uvarum et vini est. *'is the god of grapes and wine.'*

HERMES

....

Help point:

bellum = war
bestia = wild animal
dea = goddess
deus = god
geminus = twin
matrona = married woman
Musa = Muse
negotium, i, n = business
nuntius = messenger
patronus = patron
poeta = poet
sapientia = wisdom
silva = forest
tonitruum = thunder (-storm)
uva = grape
viator = traveller
vinum = wine

unguentum
('perfume')

loculus
('moneybox')
[with Mercury holding a
money bag and his staff]

fibula
('dress pin')

1 **Cultural SNAPSHOT**

📷 SATURNALIA

Based on your resources, answer the following questions:

1. Which Roman god was Saturnalia held in honour of? …………… ……………………………

2. At what time of the year did it take place?

………………………………………………………………………………

3. What was typical of this holiday? ……………………………………

………………………………………………………………………………

………………………………………………………………………………

………………………………………………………………………………

………………………………………………………

4. What types of gifts would people give each other?

………………………………………………………………………………

………………………………………………………………………………

5. Which modern celebrations does it remind you of? ………………………………………………

☆ ☆ ☆ ☆ ☆

2 Metella has started her early preparations for Saturnalia. Here is her gift **'shopping' list**:

⇒ **Who** is she planning presents **for?** Write down the translations (as in the example). ☆ ☆ ☆ ☆

a. Tito marito   *for Titus, (her) husband* ………………………

b. Tito filio   ……………………………………………

c. Pomponiae filiae ……………………………………………

d. Helviae amicae ……………………………………………

e. coquis   ……………………………………………

f. ancillis   ……………………………………………

g. tibicinis   ……………………………………………

h. servis   ……………………………………………

3 Here are some presents Metella has in mind: **who are they for?**

⇒ Use the information in 2 above and label the gift tags in Latin (as in e.g.).

e.g.

TITO
MARITO

☆ ☆ ☆ ☆

Real Lives FACT FILE 1: A Roman pet dog

Location: Getty Museum, USA   ⭐ ⭐ ⭐

Name: ....

Breed: ....

....

Origin: ....

Date: ....

Dedication: ....

....

....

....

Interpretations:

....

....

....

CUI? *('who to?')*

↱ **YOUR TURN:** Here is a **dedication**   ④
relief to Marcus's pet cockerel.

⇒   Help **design the inscription for it:**

⭐ ⭐
⭐ ⭐

Help point:

cockerel
= gallus

beloved
= amatus

pet =
deliciae (pl.)

---

5   ⇒   **Turn the names of the gods** below **into dedications** and translate them (as in the examples).

⇒   **Design appropriate votive inscriptions for** six of the dedications (as in the example).   10 ⭐

E.g.

Luna	Lunae	*'To Luna'*	Asklepius	Asklepio	*'To Asklepius'*
a. Diana	....	....	e. Bacchus	....	....
b. Hygeia	....	....	f. Mercurius	....	....
c. Minerva	....	....	g. Silvanus	....	....
d. Bellona	....	....	h. Ianus	....	....

E.g.

For YOU:
Stonemasons often made mistakes. The materials and services of a *quadratarius* to make a draft were expensive, and the engraver could still make a mistake through negligence or ignorance. Here are the instructions Sidonius, a Roman author, gives about the inscription for the grave of his grandfather:

'... watch that the mason does not make a mistake on the stone. When that happens the malignant reader will ascribe it to me, as either deliberately done or from carelessness, rather than to the cutter himself.'

pagina XIX

LUDUS et LUDI ('School and the Games')

★ ★ ☆

1 Connect the main characters from the graffiti with their names. Use the information in your text book to help you.

Hilarus   **Gallus**   **Bullarius**   **Luxurius**   **Crispinus**   **Mica**   **Furius**

The *bestiae* ('wild animals') were often named: e.g. **Mica** ('gold dust')

2 **Here are the graffiti from the wall of *ludus bestiarum*:** Using the 'Help Point' in your textbook:

  a. **Transcribe** the text (as in the example).

  b. **Translate** the phrases (as in the example).

★ ★ ★ ★ ★ ★   QUO? *('what with?')*

a SAGITTIS VVLNERATVS LVXVRIVS

SAGITTIS VULNERATUS LUXURIUS
'Luxurius wounded with arrows.'

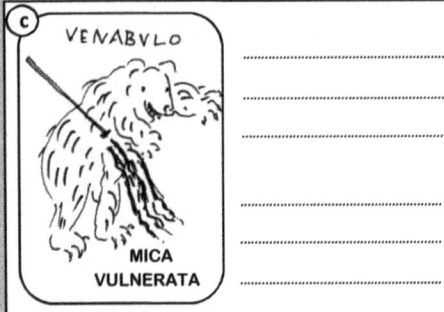

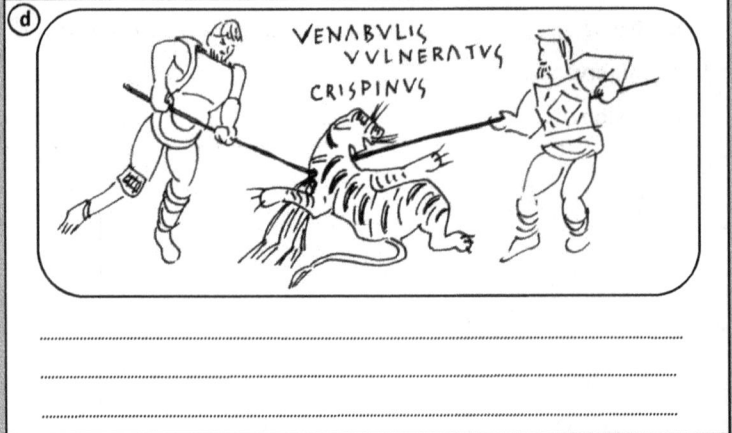

b FVRIVS VENABVLO VVLNERATVS
....
....
....
....

c VENABVLO
....
....
....
....
MICA VULNERATA
....

d VENABVLIS VVLNERATVS CRISPINVS
....
....
....

e
HILARVS PLVMBATA
....
....
....
....

f GALLVS VENABVLO
....
....
....
....

g BVLLARIVS VENABVLIS
....
....
....
....

3 Use the 'Help point' to **translate** the following phrases **into Latin** as in the example:

e.g. 'with wisdom' **sapientia** ☆ ☆ ☆ ☆

a. 'with a pen' ....

b. 'with a spear' ....

c. 'with a chisel' ....

d. 'with a mallet' ....

e. 'with arrows'...................................

f. 'with darts' ....

g. 'with swords' ....

h. 'with hunting spears' ....

> **Help point:**
>
> **English → Latin**
> *arrow* = sagitta
> *chisel* = scalprum
> *dart* = plumbata
> *hunting spear* = venabulum
> *mallet* = malleus
> *pen* = penna
> *spear* = hasta
> *sword* = gladius
>
> **Latin → English**
> bestiarius = animal handler
> caelator = engraver
> laboro, 1 = I work
> ferio, 4 = I strike
> scriba = a scribe
> scribo, 3 = I write
> venator = hunter

4 **Here are some pictures showing people and gods using different instruments.**

a. Use the Latin forms from 3 above to **fill in the gaps**.

b. **Translate** the sentences. ☆ ☆ ☆ ☆ ☆ ☆

E.g.

1. Scriba ......*penna*...... scribit.
   ....'The secretary is writing...................
   ....**with a pen.**...................

2. Caelator ....

et ....

laborat.

....

....

....

....

3. Minerva

....

ferit.

....

....

....

4. Diana .... ferit.

....

....

....

5. Bestiarii ....,

gladiatores .... **pugnant**.

....

....

6. Venator .... ferit.

....

....

....

5 ⇒ What English words come from these Latin words?

penna ☆
....

scalprum ☆
....

malleus ☆
....

laboro ☆
....

scribo ☆
....

⇒ Which Latin word do you associate with this picture and why? ☆

....

....

....

ROMAN **G**LADIATORS

Based on your resources, answer the following questions:

Roman games, coin ca. 240 AD

1. What was the origin of gladiatorial shows? ....
....
....

2. When did the first gladiatorial shows take place? ....

3. Where did gladiatorial shows take place before the building of the first amphitheatres?
....

4. What sources are there about the way gladiators were armed and dressed? ....
....
....

5. Who became a gladiator? ....
....

6. Why was it worth being a gladiator? ....
....

7. Were gladiators always killed? Why? ....
....

8. Who was *lanista*?
....
....
....
....

9. What was *rudis*? ....
....

10. What types of gladiator do you know of? ....
....

10

Real Lives FACT FILE 2: Gladiator trainers

Location: John Hopkins Archaeological Museum, Maryland

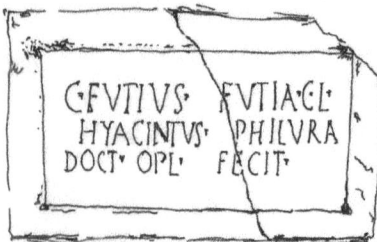

Name: ....
....
....
Job title: ....
....

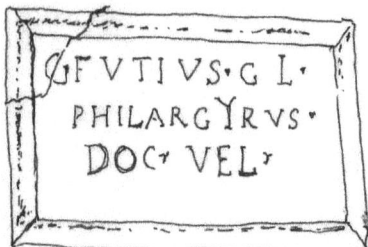

Name: ....
....
....
Job title: ....
....

Connection: ....

EXTRA 4 ☆ ☆ ☆ ☆ ☆ ☆

2

YOUR TURN: Draw your own **gladiator**.

'Parallel Lives' Book 1: REVISION SHEET 1

A   LANGUAGE FOCUS   **B**

1. Observe all the **personal names** we have come across so far. What two main **patterns** emerge?

FEMALE NAMES	MALE NAMES
Pomponia	Marcus
Aspasia	Titus
Eugenia	Eugenius
Lemnia	Euporus
Artemisia	Eutychus

2. The **same patterns** apply to other words describing men and women (e.g. **nationalities**, **occupations**).

female	*male*
puella, femina	paedagogus, philosophus
ancilla, tibicina	sumptuarius, dominus
Romana, Graeca	Romanus, Graecus

☀ In Latin we very often can guess the *gender* of a noun by its ending: -a for *feminine*, -us for *masculine*.

Observe what changes occur when **more than one person** is involved in a story.

femina	feminae
ancilla	ancillae
Graeca	Graecae

philosophus	philosophi
Graecus	Graeci
dominus	domini
Romanus	Romani

☀ In Latin we can guess the *gender* of a noun even when it is *plural*, again by its ending: -ae for *feminine*, -i for *masculine*.

TASK 1:

Translate these sentences into English.

1.   **Puella sum.** ....

2.   **Ancilla es.** ....

3.   **Dominus est.** ....

4.   **Puellae sumus.** ....

5.   **Coqui non estis.** ....

6.   **Servi sunt.** ....

7.   **Marcus puer est.** ....

8.   **Pomponia puella Romana est.** ....

9.   **Domini Romani sunt.** ....

10.   **Ancillae Romanae non sunt.** ....

C   ***ESSE 'to be'***

Singular	Plural:
1. **sum** 'I am'	1. **sumus** 'we are'
2. **es** 'you are'	2. **estis** 'you are'
3. **est** 'he/she is'	3. **sunt** 'they are'

TASK 2:   Turn the words into their plural forms, then translate (as in the examples):

Singular:	Plural:	Singular:	Plural:
1. ancilla *maid*	1. *ancillae maids*	1. dominus *master*	1. *domini masters*
2. femina	2.	2. equus	2. ....
3. puella	3.	3. deus	3. ....
4. serva	4.	4. coquus	4. ....
5. regina	5.	5. gladius	5. ....

All Latin verb forms we have come across so far are in the **Present tense**.

Note how the same **Latin verb form can be translated in two different ways in English**, depending on the context.

This is very important to **bear in mind when doing translation work!**

LANGUAGE FOCUS

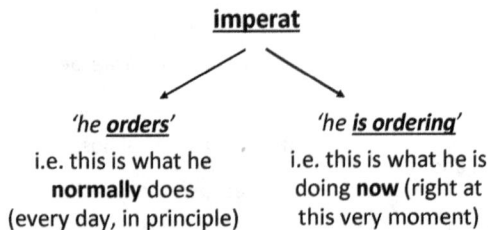

imperat

'he **orders**'
i.e. this is what he **normally** does (every day, in principle)

'he **is ordering**'
i.e. this is what he is doing **now** (right at this very moment)

Latin has one **Present tense** where English has two!

Olivae **florent**.

1. 'Olive trees **blossom**.'
i.e. this is what they usually do (every year, in principle)

2. 'The olive trees **are blossoming**.'
i.e. they are in flower now (this month / this season)

TASK 1:

Translate these sentences into English.

1. **Puella ambulat.** ....

2. **Ancilla dormit.** ....

3. **In regia habito.** ....

4. **In ludo laboramus.** ....

5. **Coqui gaudent.** ....

6. **Ubi habitas?** ....

7. **Marcus edit.** ....

8. **Pomponia in horto ridet.** ....

9. **Domini in foro ambulant.** ....

10. **Graeci cum Troianis pugnant.** ....

11. **Aeneas cum Troianis e Troia fugit.** ....

VERBS:

1. Latin **verbs** are divided in **4 groups**:

ambulo, ambul**are**,	**1**
gaudeo, gaud**ere**,	**2**
bibo, bib**ĕre**,	**3**
dormio, dorm**ire**,	**4**

2. The **verb endings** tell us who is the **person** doing the action:

Singular	Plural:
1. - **o** = 'I'	1. - **mus** = 'we'
2. - **s** = 'you'	2. - **tis** = 'you'
3. - **t** = 'he/she'	3. - **nt** = 'they'

TASK 2:

Use the **VERB MONSTER** here!

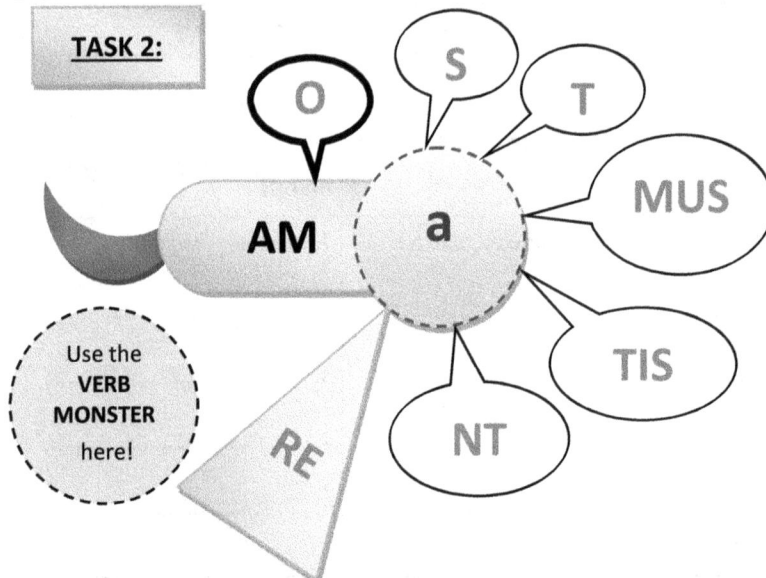

Fill in the endings and **translate:**

Sg. 1.	am	*love*
2.	ama	*love*
3.	ama	*love*
Pl. 1.	ama	*love*
2.	ama	*love*
3.	ama	*love*
Inf.	ama	*love*

LANGUAGE FOCUS

BELONGING and **POSSESSION**

In Latin belonging and possession are expressed by specific endings:

Masculine: (sg.)	Feminine: (sg.)
-i:	**-ae:**
filius Marc**i**	ancilla Metell**ae**
'Marcus's son / the son of Marcus'	*'Metella's maid / the maid of Metella'*

LANGUAGE FOCUS

BELONGING and **POSSESSION**

Note the new set of endings when the words expressing belonging or possession are in **plural**:

Masculine: (pl.)	Feminine: (pl.)
-orum:	**-arum:**
dux Troian**orum**	cella ancill**arum**
'leader of the Trojans	*'the room of the maids'*

3 Translate:

dea femin**arum**

....

culina coqu**orum**

....

domina ancill**arum**

....

regina Troian**orum**

....

1 Write down and translate the *'of' forms* (*sg.*) of the words below (as in the examples).

a. ancilla → ancill**ae** *'of the maid'*   e. coquus → coqu**i** *'of the cook'*

b. puella → ....   f. servus → ....

c. regina → ....   g. dominus → ....

d. dea → ....   h. deus → ....

2 Use the forms you made in 1. to label the pictures, then translate in two ways (as in the example):

fibula ....
'the broach ....

speculum ....
'the mirror ....
....

ligulae **coqui**

'the ladles of the cook'

'the cook's ladles'

liber ....
'the book ....
....

furca ....
'the pitchfork ....

4 Translate these sentences into English.

1. **Amica ancillae Graeca est.** ....
....

2. **Domina servi Romana est.** ....
....

3. **Culina coquorum magna non est.** ....
....

4. **Diana dea feminarum est.** ....
....

LANGUAGE FOCUS

Note how in Latin to express
TO or FOR whom

we do things, a set of specific endings is used :

	singular	plural
Masculine:	Feminine:	Both m & f
-o	**-ae**	**-is**
Aesculapi**o**	Rubr**ae**	de**is**
'to Asclepius'	*'for Rubra'*	*'to/for the gods'*

5. **Titulus magnus deo est.** ....

6. **Titulus novus dominae est.** ....

7. **Servi optime dominis laborant.** ....
....

8. **Magister Graecus puellis non placet.** ....
....

9. **Amica ancillae dominis non placet.** ....
....

A   **LANGUAGE FOCUS**   **B**

1. Observe how **some nouns** are neither masculine nor feminine:

venabulum

scutum

2. Such nouns are in fact **neuter**.

3. Typical for them is the ending **–um**.

In Latin to express that something is used as an **INSTRUMENT WITH** or **BY MEANS OF** which something is done, again a set of specific endings is used :

	singular		plural
	masculine &	feminine:	all three
	-o	**-a**	**-is**
	Gladiator gladio et scuto pugnat	Retiarius fascina pugnat.	gladiatores fascinis et gladiis vulnerati
	'A gladiator fights **with** a sword and a shield.'	'A retiarius fights **with** a trident.'	'gladiators wounded **by** tridents and swords'

N.B. The same endings are used after some prepositions, such as **cum, de, ex, in.**

3   ⇒ What English words come from these Latin words?

scribo

....

amica

....

equus

....

femina

....

navigo

....

---

1   **Delete** the wrong noun form, then translate (as in the examples).

Extra vocabulary:
hasta, ae, f—spear
penna, ae, f — a pen
scriba, ae, m — a scribe

a. Gladiator *gladio* / ~~gladius~~ pugnat.   'A gladiator fights **with a sword**.'

b. Bestiarius *venabulum / venabulo* pugnat.   '...'

c. Diana *sagittis / sagitae* pugnat.   '...'

d. Scribae *pennarum / pennis* scribunt.   '...'

e. Minerva *hasta / hastae* pugnat.   '...'

---

2   **Translate these sentences into English:**

Extra vocabulary:
bestiarius, -i, m - beast figher
coquo, 3 - I cook
furca, ae, f - pitchfork
ligula, ae, f - ladle
Murmillo - Murmillo
(type of gladiator)
parmula, ae, f - small shield
scriba, ae, m - scribe
se protegit - defends himself
Thraex - Thracian
(type of gladiator)

1. Coquus ligula coquit. ....

....

2. Servus furca laborat. ....

....

3. Scriba penna scribit. ....

....

FVRIVS
VENABVL
VVLNERA

4. Bestiarius venabulo pugnat. ....

5. Thraex parmula se protegit. ....

6. Murmillo scuto se protegit. ....

7. Gladiatores gladiis pugnant. ....

8. Marcus et Titus in ludo student; gladiis non pugnant. ....

....

9. Servus et ancilla domi laborant; venabulis non pugnant. ....

....

10. Pomponia et Aspasia domi dormiunt; scutis se non protegunt. ....

....

'Parallel Lives' Book 1: REVISION SHEET 5

Imagine you are <u>a Roman boy who goes to school</u>.

⇒ What do you like and dislike about school life?

You could include:

- at what time of the day and how you get to school
- subjects and stories you study
- tools and materials you use for writing
- discipline

'Parallel Lives' Book 1: REVISION SHEET 6

Imagine you are <u>a Roman girl helping mum get ready for Saturnalia</u>.

⇒   What do you like and dislike about this celebration?

You could include:

- the time of year
- what is unusual compared to everyday behaviour
- atmosphere and festivities
- gifts

....

....

....

....

....

....

....

....

....

....

....

....

....

....

Vitae Parallelae

(Parallel Lives)

Liber Primus
ad exercendum

(Workbook One)

Index verborum currens

(running vocabulary list)

A

ambulo, ambulare, 1 = I walk
amica, ae, f = friend (*f*)
amicus, i, m = friend (*m*)
ancilla, ae, f = maid

B

bellum, i, n = war
bene = well; well done!
bestia, ae, f = wild animal
bestiarius, i, m = animal handler
bibo, bibere, 3 = I drink

C

caelator = engraver
canto, 1 = I sing
caseus = cheese
ceterus = other, the rest
cogito, 1 = I think
coquus, i, m = cook
Cuius...? = Whose?
culina, ae, f = kitchen

D

de = from; about
dea, ae, f = goddess
deinde = then / after that
deus, i, m = god
dico, 3 = I say
discipulus, i, m = pupil
diu = for a long time
diu = for a long time
domi = at home
domina, ae, f = mistrees
dominus, i, m = master
dormio, 4 = I sleep

E

e (ex) = out of
Ecce! = Look! Behold!
edo, edere, 3 = I eat
ego = I
equus, i, m = horse
ergo = therefore
esurio, 4 = I am hungry
et = and
Euge! = Hooray!
ex = out of

F

femina, ae, f = woman
ferio, 4 = I strike
filia, ae, f = daughter
filius, i, m = son
forum, i, n = market place
fugio, fugere, 3 = I run away

G

gallina, ae, f = hen
gallus, i, m = cockerel
gaudeo, 2 = I rejoice
geminus = twin
gladius, i, m = sword
Graecus = Greek

H

habito, 1 = I live

I

impero, 1 = I order, command
in = in / on
in horto = in the garden
in ludo = at school
in regia = in the palace
intelligo, intelligere 3 = I understand
invenio, 4 = I find
ita = yes, so
Ithaca, ae, f = the island of Ithaca

L

laboro, 1 = I work
lac = milk
lacrimo, 1 = I cry
lateo, 2 = I hide
libertus, i, m = freedman
ligneus = wooden
Luna, ae, f = the Moon

M

magister, magistri, m = teacher
magistra, ae, f = teacher (*f*)
magnus = big, great
matrona, ae, f = married woman
meus = my
minime = no
Musa, ae, f = Muse

N

natura, ae, f = nature
navigo, navigare, 1 = I sail
negotium, i, n = business
novus = new
nunc = now
nuntius, i, m = messenger

O

oleo, 2 = I smell
oliva, ae, f = olive
optime = excellent!

P

patronus, i, m = patron
pecunia, ae, f = money
Penelope = Penelope
per = through
placeo, 2 = I am pleasing
poeta, ae, m = poet
porcus, i, n = pig
puella, ae, f = girl
puer, i, m = boy
pugno, 1 = I fight

Q

Quid...? = What...?
Quis...? = Who...?
quoque = also

R

regina, ae, f = queen
rideo, 2 = I laugh
ripa, ae, f = (sea)shore

S

sagitta, ae, f = arrow
Salve! = 'Hello!'
sapientia, ae, f = wisdom
scriba, ae, f = scribe, secretary
scribo, scribere, 3 = I write
scutum, i, n = shield
sed = but
serva, ae, f = slave (*f.*)

servus, i, m = slave (*m.*)

silva, ae, f = forest

sitio, 4 = I am thirsty

spelunca, ae, f = cave

splendeo, 2 = I shine

stella, ae, f = star

T

tempus = time

tonitruum = thunder (-storm)

Troia, ae, f = Troy

Troianus = (a) Trojan

tu = you (sg.)

U

Ubi...? = Where...?

uva, ae, f = (bunch of) grapes

V

venabulum, i, n = hunting spear

venator = hunter

venio, 4 = I come

via, ae, f = street; journey; way; path

viator = traveller

vinum, i, n = wine

volo, velle = I want

vos = you (pl.)